The Natural History Museu

Animal Close-U

Sea Creatures

Barbara Taylor

PETER BEDRICK BOOKS

McGraw-Hill
Children's Publishing

A Division of The **McGraw·Hill** *Companies*

Published in the United States in 2002 by
Peter Bedrick Books, an imprint of
McGraw-Hill Children's Publishing,
A Division of The McGraw-Hill Companies
8787 Orion Place
Columbus, OH 43240

www.MHkids.com

ISBN 1-57768-969-0

Library of Congress Cataloging-in-Publication Data is on file with the publisher.

Text copyright © Barbara Taylor 2002
Photographs copyright © The Natural History Museum, London 2002
Photographs by Frank Greenaway

The moral rights of the author have been asserted

Database right Oxford University Press (maker)

First published 2002 in arrangement with Oxford University Press.

1 3 5 7 9 10 8 6 4 2

Printed in Hong Kong

Contents

About this book
This book takes a close look at fish and other
animals that live in the sea or on the shore.
It shows how their body shapes help them to feed,
move, and survive in a world of water.

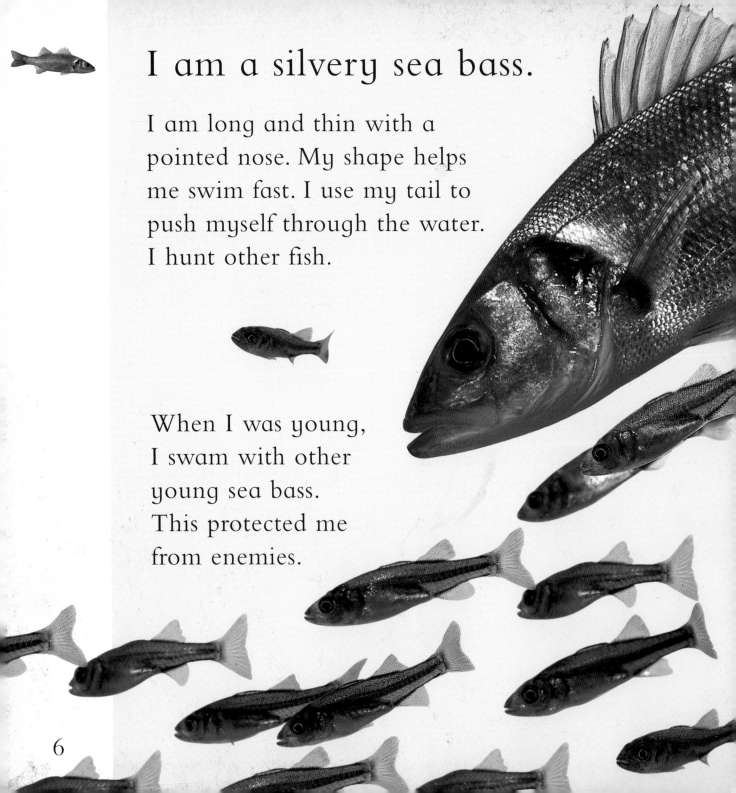

I am a silvery sea bass.

I am long and thin with a
pointed nose. My shape helps
me swim fast. I use my tail to
push myself through the water.
I hunt other fish.

When I was young,
I swam with other
young sea bass.
This protected me
from enemies.

6

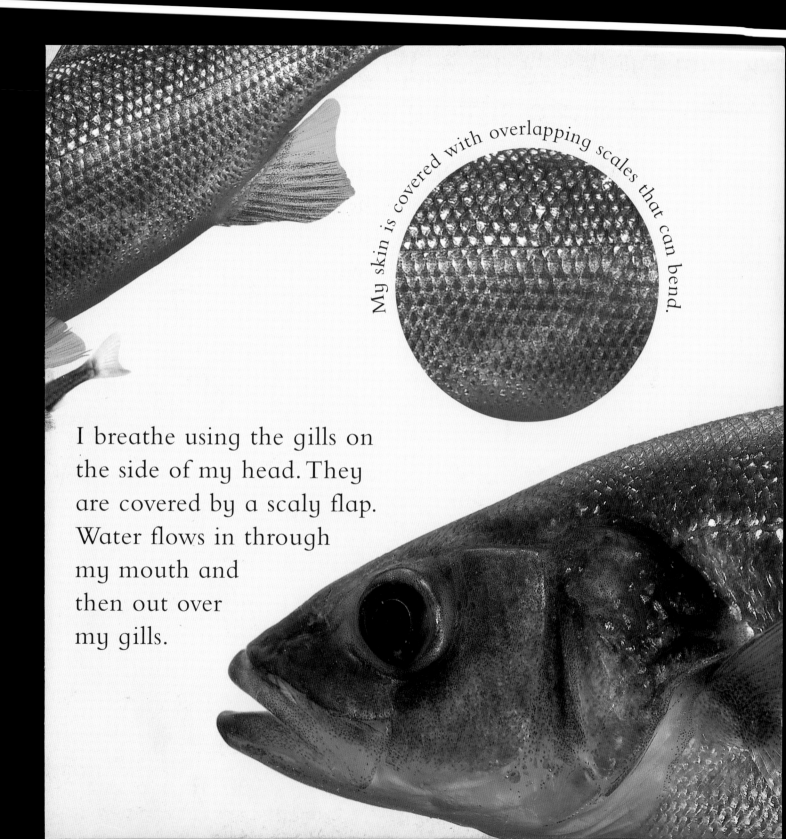

My skin is covered with overlapping scales that can bend.

I breathe using the gills on the side of my head. They are covered by a scaly flap. Water flows in through my mouth and then out over my gills.

I am a bright yellow tang.

I live on coral reefs in warm oceans. I have two sharp spines near my tail. I lash my tail from side to side to cut my enemies' flesh.

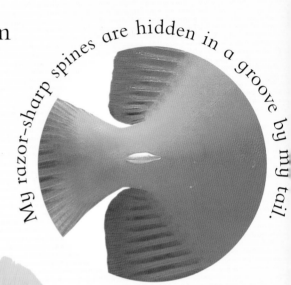

My razor-sharp spines are hidden in a groove by my tail.

I use my small biting teeth to scrape plants off coral and rocks.

My deep, oval body is very flat. I use my fins for balance.

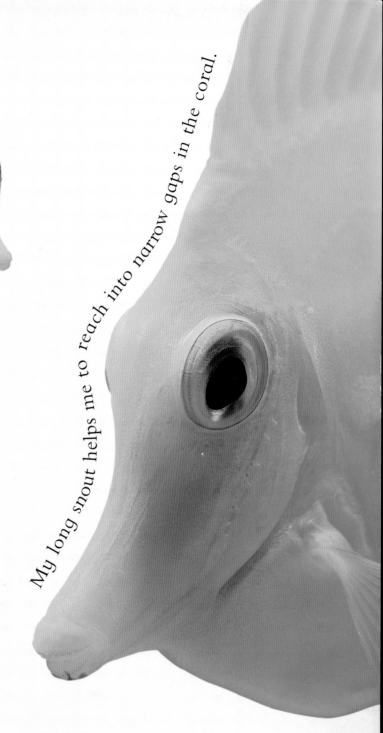

My long snout helps me to reach into narrow gaps in the coral.

I breathe through gills just behind my eyes.

I am a speckled flatfish.

I am called a top knot. My fins are around the edge of my flat body. My underside is pale, with rows of muscles. They help me to swim.

My top side is brown, with spots and blotches that help me blend in with sand and gravel on the sea bed.

My eyes are both on the same side of my head – the top.

I am a spotted pufferfish.

I live in warm seas. I do
not have scales, but my
skin is bumpy.

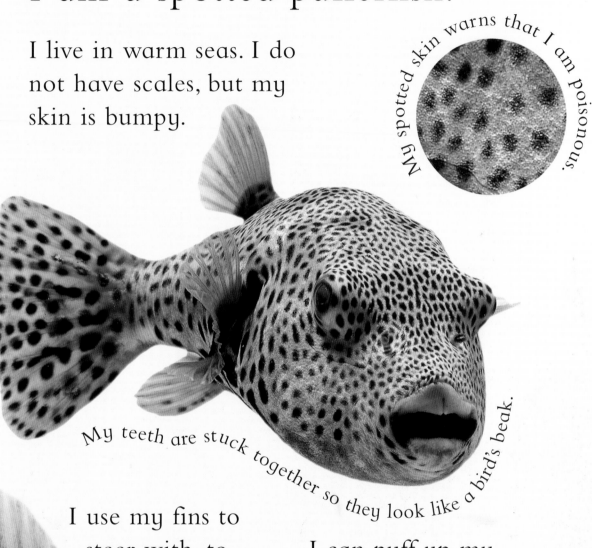

My spotted skin warns that I am poisonous.

My teeth are stuck together so they look like a bird's beak.

I use my fins to
steer with, to
balance, and
to slow down.

I can puff up my
body with water or
air, so my enemies
cannot swallow me.

I am a leafy sea dragon.

I am a kind of pipefish,
but the strange flaps
all over my body make
me look like seaweed.
It is hard for enemies
to spot me with such
a clever disguise!

My body is covered
with bony plates.
There are knobs and
spines where the plates
fit together.

This is what the plates look like in close-up.

I suck up shrimp
with my long,
tube-like jaws.

I am a stinging sea anemone.

I might look a little like a flower, but I am an animal. I sit on rocks and wait for my food to pass by. I eat small fish and other creatures. I catch them in my waving tentacles.

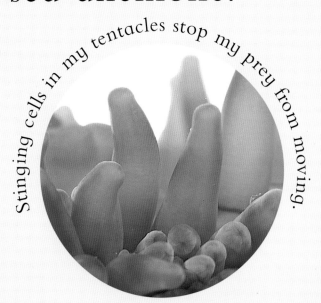

Stinging cells in my tentacles stop my prey from moving.

When I pull in my tentacles, I look like a blob of jelly.

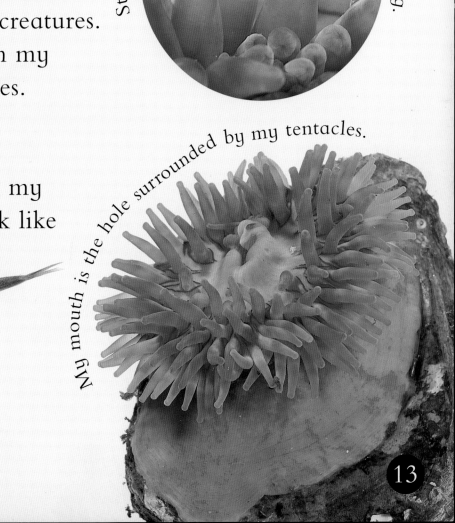

My mouth is the hole surrounded by my tentacles.

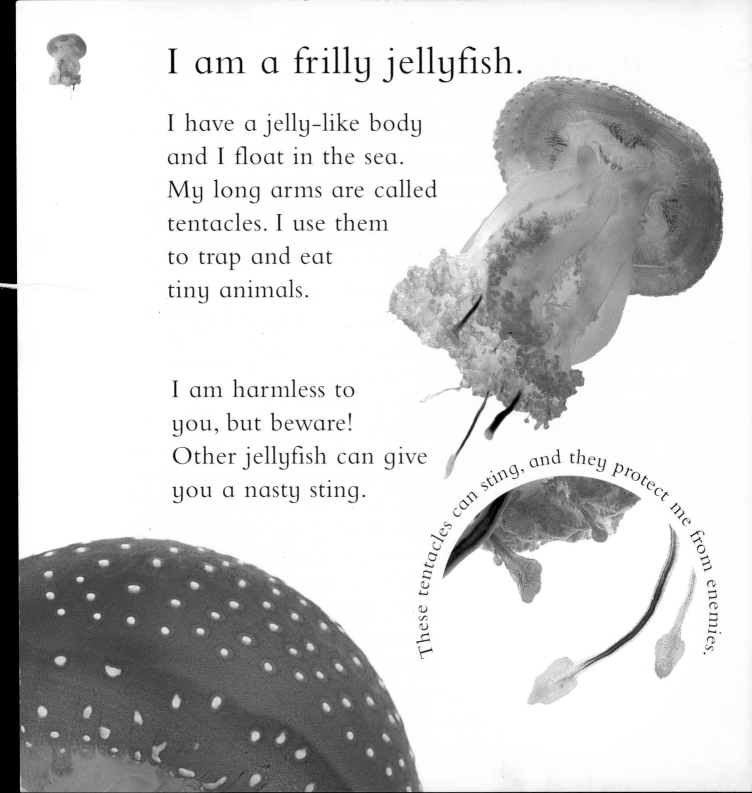

I am a frilly jellyfish.

I have a jelly-like body
and I float in the sea.
My long arms are called
tentacles. I use them
to trap and eat
tiny animals.

I am harmless to
you, but beware!
Other jellyfish can give
you a nasty sting.

These tentacles can sting, and they protect me from enemies.

I am a snappy scallop.

I swim by clapping the two halves of my shell together. I can shoot backwards very fast to escape from danger.

The rows of black dots along the edge of my shell are my eyes.

The ridges on my shell make it very strong.

The two halves of my shell are joined at the back. Each half is called a

I am a scuttling crab.

My hard skeleton is on the
outside of my body. I have
to shed, or molt, my
skeleton in order
to grow.

I use my pincers to attack my enemies and eat my food.

My legs are made up of seven parts, with joints between them.

I have eight walking legs and two big pincers. My tail is folded under my body.

I have two pairs of antennae, which help me sense food.

17

I am a squirming octopus.

I have eight long arms
with rows of suckers along
them. I curl my arms
around my prey.

I am not quite as big as my picture on this page.

I use my arms for
swimming, feeding,
and fighting. I eat
my food using my
beak-like jaws.

18

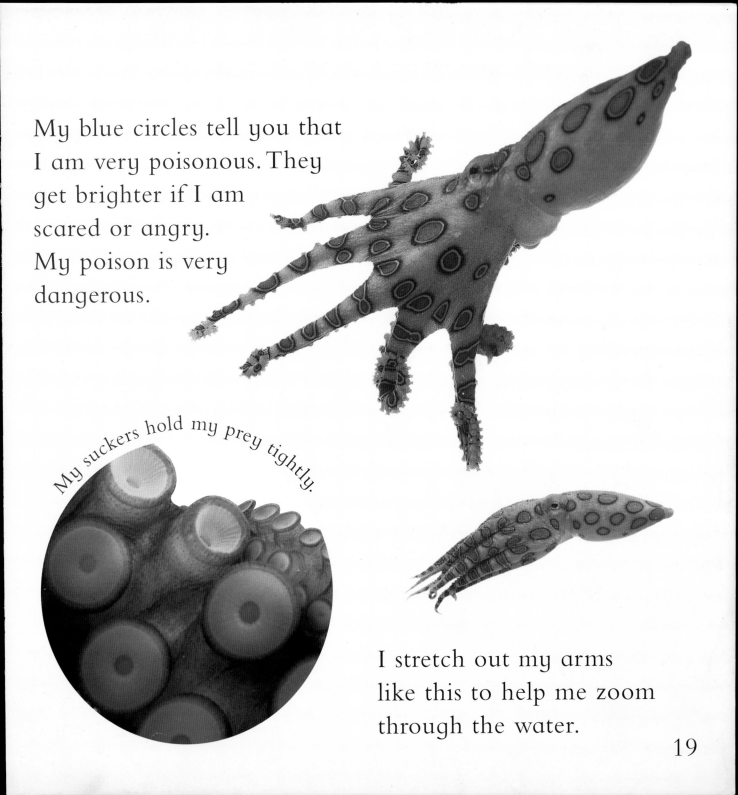

My blue circles tell you that I am very poisonous. They get brighter if I am scared or angry. My poison is very dangerous.

My suckers hold my prey tightly.

I stretch out my arms like this to help me zoom through the water.

19

I am a spiny starfish.

I have five flexible arms that bend. If one of my arms is crushed or bitten off, I can grow a new one.

My tough skin and spines help to support and protect my body.

Under my arms are rows of tiny tube feet, full of water. I use these feet to glide along and to pull open the shellfish that I eat.

20

I can pump water into my feet, which makes them longer.

Sunstars have more legs than I do. How many legs does this one have?

I need to keep my body damp. If I am washed up on the beach, I will dry out. At low tide, I creep under rocks or hide in rock pools.

Glossary

gills A collection of thin flaps that allow fish and some young amphibians to breathe under water.

molting The shedding of the outer covering of an animal's body, which allows it to grow.

scales Thin, hard, overlapping plates that protect the skin of fish and reptiles.

skeleton A strong framework that supports an animal's body.

tentacle A long flexible structure like an arm, near an animal's mouth. It may have suckers or stings.

valve One half of the two-part shell of a shellfish, such as a scallop.